From
Aunt Dot & Uncle Bo[...]

this book belongs to
Barbara Lockard

FAVORITE
INSPIRATIONAL POEMS

FAVORITE INSPIRATIONAL POEMS

Poetic Selections from All Ages

FLEMING H. REVELL COMPANY

OLD TAPPAN • NEW JERSEY

COPYRIGHT © MCMLX BY FLEMING H. REVELL COMPANY
All rights reserved

Library of Congress Catalog Card Number: 60-13101

ISBN 0-8007-1143-2

Printed in the United States of America

Acknowledgment is made to the following, who have granted permission for the reprinting of copyrighted and other material:

HODDER & STOUGHTON LTD. for "Indifference" from *The Unutterable Beauty* by G. A. Studdert-Kennedy, and for "Peace and Joy" by the same author.

CHARLES SCRIBNER'S SONS for "Four Things" from *The Builders* by Henry van Dyke, copyrighted 1897 by Charles Scribner's Sons.

MRS. WILLIAM L. STIDGER for "I Saw God Wash the World" by Dr. William L. Stidger.

The Sunday School Times for "Overheard in an Orchard" by Elizabeth Cheney, published in the issue of November 20, 1920.

FROM **ENDYMION**

A thing of beauty is a joy forever.
Its loveliness increases; it will never
Pass into nothingness; but still will keep
A bower quiet for us, and a sleep
Full of sweet dreams, and health, and quiet breathing.
JOHN KEATS

Contents

54	ALUMNUS FOOTBALL (extract),	*Grantland Rice*
34	"ANDREW RYKMAN'S PRAYER" (extract),	*John Greenleaf Whittier*
42	ANGEL UNAWARES, AN, *unknown*	
28	ANNIE LAURIE, *William Douglas*	
45	BETRAYAL, *Hester H. Cholmondeley*	
44	BIDE A WEE! *John Oxenham*	
23	BIRTHDAY, A, *Christina Rossetti*	
37	BISHOP BLOUGRAM'S APOLOGY (extract),	*Robert Browning*
43	BOOK OUR MOTHERS READ, THE,	*John Greenleaf Whittier*
57	CHAMBERED NAUTILUS, THE (extract),	*Oliver Wendell Holmes*
55	CROSSING THE BAR, *Alfred Tennyson*	
20	DAFFODILS, *William Wordsworth*	
50	DAY'S DEMAND, THE, *Josiah Gilbert Holland*	
58	DEATH, *John Donne*	
38	DEDICATION, *William Cullen Bryant*	
29	DOVER BEACH, *Matthew Arnold*	
18	EACH IN HIS OWN TONGUE,	*William Herbert Carruth*
5	ENDYMION (extract), *John Keats*	
60	EPITAPH PLACED ON HIS DAUGHTER'S TOMB BY MARK TWAIN,	adapted from *Robert Richardson*

56	ETERNAL GOODNESS, THE (extract), *John Greenleaf Whittier*
38	FAITH, *John Greenleaf Whittier*
39	FLOWER IN THE CRANNIED WALL, *Alfred Tennyson*
47	FOUR THINGS, *Henry van Dyke*
16	"GIVE US THIS DAY OUR DAILY BREAD," *Maltbie D. Babcock*
27	GO, LOVELY ROSE! *Edmund Waller*
24	HAPPY THOUGHT, *Robert Louis Stevenson*
31	HOUSE AND HOME, *Victor Hugo*
26	HOW DO I LOVE THEE?, *Elizabeth Barrett Browning*
50	I AM NOT BOUND TO WIN, *Abraham Lincoln*
35	IF, *Emily Dickinson*
46	INDIFFERENCE, *G. A. Studdert-Kennedy*
21	I NEVER SAW A MOOR, *Emily Dickinson*
48	I SAW GOD WASH THE WORLD, *William L. Stidger*
32	*JULIUS CAESAR* (extract), *William Shakespeare*
22	LAMB, THE, *William Blake*
36	LAST DEFILE, THE, *Amy Carmichael*
25	LOVE, *unknown*
14	MARSHES OF GLYNN, THE (extract), *Sidney Lanier*
47	MASTER-PLAYER, THE, *Paul Laurence Dunbar*
32	MOTHER O' MINE, *Rudyard Kipling*
61	MUSIC, WHEN SOFT VOICES DIE, *Percy Bysshe Shelley*
19	MY GARDEN, *Thomas E. Brown*
17	MY HEART LEAPS UP, *William Wordsworth*
53	NATION'S STRENGTH, A, *Ralph Waldo Emerson*
13	ODE, *Arthur William O'Shaughnessy*
60	OLD ASTRONOMER, THE (extract), *Sarah Williams*
31	"OLD, OLD SONG," THE, *Charles Kingsley*

22	ONE THOUSANDTH PSALM, THE, *Edward Everett Hale*
39	ON HIS BLINDNESS, *John Milton*
58	ON HIS SEVENTY-FIFTH BIRTHDAY, *Walter Savage Landor*
54	OUR MASTER, *John Greenleaf Whittier*
16	OUT IN THE FIELDS WITH GOD, *unknown*
36	OVERHEARD IN AN ORCHARD, *Elizabeth Cheney*
41	PEACE AND JOY, *G. A. Studdert-Kennedy*
17	PIPPA'S SONG, *Robert Browning*
44	POSSESSION, *unknown*
52	PRESENT CRISIS, THE (extract), *James Russell Lowell*
40	PREVAILING PRAYER, *Archbishop Trench*
40	PROPS, *John Oxenham*
57	RABBI BEN EZRA (extract), *Robert Browning*
51	RECESSIONAL, *Rudyard Kipling*
24	RED, RED ROSE, A, *Robert Burns*
61	REQUIEM, *Robert Louis Stevenson*
43	RETRIBUTION, *Henry Wadsworth Longfellow*
42	RIME OF THE ANCIENT MARINER, THE (extract), *Samuel Taylor Coleridge*
35	SHEPHERD BOY'S SONG, THE, *John Bunyan*
25	SINGERS, *Henry Wadsworth Longfellow*
41	SIR GALAHAD (extract), *Alfred Tennyson*
58	SIR WALTER RALEIGH'S VERSES, FOUND IN HIS BIBLE IN THE GATEHOUSE AT WESTMINSTER, *Walter Raleigh*
33	STRADIVARIUS (extract), *George Eliot*

45	THAT HOLY THING, *George Macdonald*
49	THEY THAT WAIT UPON THE LORD, *Isaiah* 40:28-31
33	TO A LOUSE (extract), *Robert Burns*
14	TO A WATERFOWL, *William Cullen Bryant*
30	TO MY WIFE, *Robert Louis Stevenson*
59	ULYSSES (extract), *Alfred Tennyson*
56	VANISHED, *Emily Dickinson*
42	WAY, THE, *Henry van Dyke*
37	WAYS, THE, *John Oxenham*
20	WHEN I HEARD THE LEARN'D ASTRONOMER, *Walt Whitman*
34	WHOSO DRAWS NIGH TO GOD, *unknown*
19	WIND, THE, *Christina Rossetti*
55	WINGS, *Victor Hugo*
52	WORLD OVER, THE, *James Russell Lowell*

FAVORITE
INSPIRATIONAL POEMS

ODE

We are the music-makers,
    And we are the dreamers of dreams,
Wandering by lone sea-breakers,
    And sitting by desolate streams;
World-losers and world-forsakers;
    On whom the pale moon gleams:
Yet we are the movers and shakers
    Of the world forever, it seems.

With wonderful deathless ditties
We build up the world's great cities,
    And out of a fabulous story
    We fashion an empire's glory:
One man with a dream, at pleasure,
    Shall go forth and conquer a crown;
And three with a new song's measure
    Can trample a kingdom down.

We, in the ages lying
    In the buried past of the earth,
Built Nineveh with our sighing,
    And Babel itself with our mirth;
And o'erthrew them with prophesying
    To the old of the new world's worth;
For each age is a dream that is dying,
    Or one that is coming to birth.

Arthur William O'Shaughnessy

From THE MARSHES OF GLYNN

Ye marshes, how candid and simple and nothing-with-
    holding and free
Ye publish yourselves to the sky and offer yourselves to
    the sea!
Tolerant plains, that suffer the sea and the rains and
    the sun,
Ye spread and span like the catholic man who hath
    mightily won
God out of knowledge and good out of infinite pain
And sight out of blindness and purity out of a stain.

As the marsh-hen secretly builds on the watery sod,
Behold I will build me a nest on the greatness of God:
I will fly in the greatness of God as the marsh-hen flies
In the freedom that fills all the space 'twixt the marsh
    and the skies:
By so many roots as the marsh-grass sends in the sod
I will heartily lay me a-hold on the greatness of God:
Oh, like to the greatness of God is the greatness within
The range of the marshes, the liberal marshes of Glynn.

Sidney Lanier

TO A WATERFOWL

    Whither, 'midst falling dew,
While glow the heavens with the last steps of day,
Far, through their rosy depths, dost thou pursue
    Thy solitary way!

    Vainly the fowler's eye
Might mark thy distant flight to do thee wrong,
As, darkly painted on the crimson sky,
    Thy figure floats along.

    Seek'st thou the plashy brink
Of weedy lake, or marge of river wide,
Or where the rocking billows rise and sink
    On the chafed ocean side?

    There is a power whose care
Teaches thy way along that pathless coast,—
The desert and illimitable air,—
    Lone wandering, but not lost.

    All day thy wings have fanned,
At that far height, the cold, thin atmosphere,
Yet stoop not, weary, to the welcome land,
    Though the dark night is near.

    And soon that toil shall end;
Soon shalt thou find a summer home, and rest,
And scream among thy fellows; reeds shall bend,
    Soon, o'er thy sheltered nest.

    Thou'rt gone, the abyss of heaven
Hath swallowed up thy form; yet, on my heart
Deeply hath sunk the lesson thou hast given,
    And shall not soon depart.

    He who, from zone to zone,
Guides through the boundless sky thy certain flight,
In the long way that I must tread alone,
    Will lead my steps aright.

William Cullen Bryant

OUT IN THE FIELDS WITH GOD

The little cares that fretted me,
   I lost them yesterday,
Among the fields above the sea,
   Among the winds at play,
Among the lowing of the herds,
   The rustling of the trees,
Among the singing of the birds,
   The humming of the bees.

The foolish fears of what might pass
   I cast them all away
Among the clover-scented grass
   Among the new-mown hay,
Among the rustling of the corn
   Where drowsy poppies nod,
Where ill thoughts die and good are born—
   Out in the fields with God!

Author unknown

"GIVE US THIS DAY OUR DAILY BREAD"

Back of the loaf is the snowy flour,
   And back of the flour the mill,
And back of the mill is the wheat and the shower,
   And the sun and the Father's will.

Maltbie D. Babcock

MY HEART LEAPS UP

My heart leaps up when I behold
   A rainbow in the sky;
So was it when my life began;
So is it now I am a man;
So be it when I shall grow old.
   Or let me die!
The Child is father of the Man;
And I could wish my days to be
Bound each to each by natural piety.

William Wordsworth

PIPPA'S SONG

   The year's at the spring,
   And day's at the morn;
   Morning's at seven;
   The hill-side's dew-pearl'd;
   The lark's on the wing;
   The snail's on the thorn;
   God's in His heaven—
   All's right with the world!

Robert Browning

EACH IN HIS OWN TONGUE

A fire-mist and a planet—
    A crystal and a cell,
A jelly-fish and a saurian,
    And caves where the cave-men dwell;
Then a sense of law and beauty
    And a face turned from the clod,—
Some call it Evolution,
    And others call it God.

A haze on the far horizon,
    The infinite, tender sky,
The ripe, rich tint of the cornfields,
    And the wild geese sailing high;
And all over upland and lowland
    The charm of the golden-rod,—
Some of us call it Autumn,
    And others call it God.

Like tides on a crescent sea-beach,
    When the moon is new and thin,
Into our hearts high yearnings
    Come welling and surging in;
Come from the mystic ocean
    Whose rim no foot has trod,—
Some of us call it Longing,
    And others call it God.

A picket frozen on duty,
    A mother starved for her brood,
Socrates drinking the hemlock,
    And Jesus on the rood;

And millions who, humble and nameless,
   The straight, hard pathway plod,—
Some call it Consecration,
   And others call it God.

William Herbert Carruth

MY GARDEN

A garden is a lovesome thing, God wot!
Rose plot,
Fringed pool,
Ferned grot—
The veriest school
Of peace; and yet the fool
Contends that God is not—
Not God! in gardens! when the eve is cool!
Nay, but I have a sign;
'Tis very sure God walks in mine.

Thomas E. Brown

THE WIND

"The wind bloweth where it listeth, but
    thou canst not tell . . ."

Who has seen the wind?
   Neither I nor you.
But when the leaves hang trembling,
   The wind is passing through.

Who has seen the wind?
    Neither you nor I.
But when the trees bow down their
    heads,
    The wind is passing by.

Christina Rossetti

WHEN I HEARD THE LEARN'D ASTRONOMER

When I heard the learn'd astronomer;
When the proofs, the figures, were ranged in columns before me;
When I was shown the charts and diagrams, to add, divide, and measure them;
When I, sitting, heard the astronomer, where he lectured with much applause in the lecture-room,
How soon, unaccountable, I became tired and sick;
Till rising and gliding out, I wander'd off by myself,
In the mystical moist night-air, and from time to time,
Look'd up in perfect silence at the stars.

Walt Whitman

DAFFODILS

I wandered lonely as a cloud
    That floats on high o'er vales and hills,
When all at once I saw a crowd,
    A host, of golden daffodils;
Beside the lake, beneath the trees,
Fluttering and dancing in the breeze.

Continuous as the stars that shine
   And twinkle on the Milky Way,
They stretched in never-ending line
   Along the margin of a bay:
Ten thousand saw I at a glance,
Tossing their heads in sprightly dance.

The waves beside them danced, but they
   Out-did the sparkling waves in glee:
A poet could not but be gay,
   In such a jocund company:
I gazed—and gazed—but little thought
   What wealth the show to me had brought:

For oft, when on my couch I lie
   In vacant or in pensive mood,
They flash upon that inward eye
   Which is the bliss of solitude;
And then my heart with pleasure fills,
   And dances with the daffodils.

William Wordsworth

I NEVER SAW A MOOR

I never saw a moor,
I never saw the sea;
Yet know I how the heather looks,
And what a wave must be.

I never spoke with God,
Nor visited in heaven;
Yet certain am I of the spot
As if the chart were given.

Emily Dickinson

THE LAMB

Little Lamb, who made thee?
Dost thou know who made thee?
Gave thee life, and bid thee feed,
By the stream and o'er the mead;
Gave thee clothing of delight,
Softest clothing, woolly, bright;
Gave thee such a tender voice,
Making all the vales rejoice?
Little Lamb, who made thee?
Dost thou know who made thee?

Little Lamb, I'll tell thee,
Little Lamb, I'll tell thee:
He is callèd by thy name,
For He calls Himself a Lamb.
He is meek, and He is mild;
He became a little child.
I a child, and thou a lamb,
We are callèd by His name.
Little Lamb, God bless thee!
Little Lamb, God bless thee!

William Blake

THE ONE THOUSANDTH PSALM

O God, we thank Thee for everything.
For the sea and its waves, blue, green and gray and always wonderful;
For the beach and the breakers and the spray and the white foam on the rocks;

For the blue arch of heaven; for the clouds in the sky,
    white and gray and purple;
For the green of the grass; for the forests in their spring
    beauty; for the wheat and corn and rye and barley.
We thank Thee for all Thou hast made and that Thou
    hast called it good;
For all the glory and beauty and wonder of the world.
We thank Thee that Thou hast placed us in the world
    to subdue all things to Thy glory,
And to use all things for the good of Thy children.

Edward Everett Hale

A BIRTHDAY

My heart is like a singing bird
    Whose heart is in a watered shoot:
My heart is like an apple-tree
    Whose boughs are bent with thickset fruit;

My heart is like a rainbow shell
    That paddles in a halcyon sea;
My heart is gladder than all these
    Because my love is come to me.

Raise me a dais of silk and down;
    Hang it with vair and purple dyes;
Carve it in doves and pomegranates,
    And peacocks with a hundred eyes;

Work it in gold and silver grapes,
    In leaves and silver fleurs-de-lys;
Because the birthday of my life
    Is come, my love is come to me.

Christina Rossetti

HAPPY THOUGHT

The world is so full
    Of a number of things,
I'm sure we should all
    Be as happy as kings.

Robert Louis Stevenson

A RED, RED ROSE

O my Luve's like a red, red rose,
    That's newly sprung in June:
O my Luve's like the melodie
    That's sweetly play'd in tune.

As fair art thou, my bonnie lass,
    So deep in luve am I;
And I will luve thee still, my dear,
    Till a' the seas gang dry.

Till a' the seas gang dry, my dear,
    And the rocks melt wi' the sun;
And I will luve thee still, my dear,
    While the sands o' life shall run.

And fare thee weel, my only Luve!
    And fare thee weel awhile!
And I will come again, my Luve,
    Tho' it were ten thousand mile.

Robert Burns

SINGERS

God sent His singers upon earth
With songs of gladness and of mirth,
That they might touch the hearts of men,
And bring them back to heaven again.

Henry Wadsworth Longfellow

LOVE

I love you,
Not only for what you are,
But for what I am
When I am with you.

I love you,
Not only for what
You have made of yourself,
But for what
You are making of me.

I love you
For the part of me
That you bring out;
I love you
For putting your hand
Into my heaped-up heart
And passing over
All the foolish, weak things
That you can't help
Dimly seeing there,
And for drawing out
Into the light

All the beautiful belongings
That no one else had looked
Quite far enough to find.

I love you because you
Are helping me to make
Of the lumber of my life
Not a tavern
But a temple;
Out of the works
Of my every day
Not a reproach
But a song. . . .

Author unknown

HOW DO I LOVE THEE?

How do I love thee? Let me count the ways.
I love thee to the depth and breadth and height
My soul can reach, when feeling out of sight
For the ends of Being and ideal Grace.
I love thee to the level of everyday's
Most quiet need, by sun and candle-light.
I love thee freely, as men strive for Right;
I love thee purely, as they turn from Praise.
I love thee with the passion put to use
In my old griefs, and with my childhood's faith.
I love thee with a love I seemed to lose
With my lost saints—I love thee with the breath,
Smiles, tears, of all my life!—and, if God choose,
I shall but love thee better after death.

Elizabeth Barrett Browning

GO, LOVELY ROSE!

Go, lovely Rose!
Tell her that wastes her time and me
That now she knows,
When I resemble her to thee,
How sweet and fair she seems to be.

Tell her that's young,
And shun to have her graces spied,
That hadst thou sprung
In deserts, where no men abide,
Thou must have uncommended died.

Small is the worth
Of beauty from the light retired;
Bid her come forth,
Suffer herself to be desired,
And not blush so to be admired.

Then die! that she
The common fate of all things rare
May read in thee;
How small a part of time they share
That are so wondrous sweet and fair!

Edmund Waller

ANNIE LAURIE

Maxwelton's braes are bonnie
Where early fa's the dew,
And it's there that Annie Laurie
Gie'd me her promise true;
Gie'd me her promise true,
Which ne'er forgot will be;
And for bonnie Annie Laurie
I'd lay me doun and dee.

Her brow is like the snaw drift;
Her throat is like the swan;
Her face it is the fairest
That e'er the sun shone on—
That e'er the sun shone on—
And dark blue is her ee;
And for bonnie Annie Laurie
I'd lay me doun and dee.

Like dew on the gowan lying
Is the fa' o' her fairy feet;
And like the winds in summer sighing,
Her voice is low and sweet—
Her voice is low and sweet—
And she's a' the world to me;
And for bonnie Annie Laurie
I'd lay me doun and dee.

William Douglas

DOVER BEACH

The sea is calm to-night.
The tide is full, the moon lies fair
Upon the straits;—on the French coast the light
Gleams and is gone; the cliffs of England stand,
Glimmering and vast, out in the tranquil bay.
Come to the window, sweet is the night-air!

Only, from the long line of spray
Where the sea meets the moon-blanch'd land,
Listen! you hear the grating roar
Of pebbles which the waves draw back, and fling,
At their return, up the high strand,
Begin, and cease, and then again begin,
With tremulous cadence slow, and bring
The eternal note of sadness in.

Sophocles long ago
Heard it on the Aegean, and it brought
Into his mind the turbid ebb and flow
Of human misery; we
Find also in the sound a thought,
Hearing it by this distant northern sea.

The Sea of Faith
Was once, too, at the full, and round earth's shore
Lay like the folds of a bright girdle furled.
But now I only hear
Its melancholy, long withdrawing roar,
Retreating, to the breath
Of the night-wind, down the vast edges drear
And naked shingles of the world.

Favorite Inspirational Poems

Ah, love, let us be true
To one another! for the world, which seems
To lie before us like a land of dreams,
So various, so beautiful, so new,
Hath really neither joy, nor love, nor light,
Nor certitude, nor peace, nor help for
    pain;
And we are here as on a darkling plain
Swept with confused alarms of struggle
    and flight,
Where ignorant armies clash by night.

Matthew Arnold

TO MY WIFE

Trusty, dusky, vivid, true,
With eyes of gold and bramble-dew,
Steel true and blade straight
The Great Artificer made my mate.

Honor, anger, valor, fire,
A love that life could never tire,
Death quench nor evil stir,
The Mighty Master gave to her.

Teacher, tender comrade, wife,
A fellow-farer true through life,
Heart-whole and soul-free,
The August Father gave to me.

Robert Louis Stevenson

HOUSE AND HOME

A house is built of logs and stone,
   Of tiles and posts and piers;
A home is built of loving deeds
   That stand a thousand years.

Victor Hugo

THE "OLD, OLD SONG"

When all the world is young, lad,
   And all the trees are green;
And every goose a swan, lad,
   And every lass a queen;
Then hey for boot and horse, lad,
   And round the world away;
Young blood must have its course, lad,
   And every dog its day.

When all the world is old, lad,
   And all the trees are brown;
And all the sport is stale, lad,
   And all the wheels run down:
Creep home, and take your place there,
   The spent and maim'd among:
God grant you find one face there
   You loved when all was young.

Charles Kingsley

MOTHER O' MINE

If I were hanged on the highest hill,
   Mother o' mine, O mother o' mine!
I know whose love would follow me still,
   Mother o' mine, O mother o' mine!
If I were drowned in the deepest sea,
   Mother o' mine, O mother o' mine!
I know whose tears would come down to me,
   Mother o' mine, O mother o' mine!
If I were damned o' body and soul,
I know whose prayers would make me whole,
   Mother o' mine, O mother o' mine!

Rudyard Kipling

From *JULIUS CAESAR*

There is a tide in the affairs of men,
Which, taken at the flood, leads on to fortune;
Omitted, all the voyage of their life
Is bound in shallows and in miseries:
And we must take the current when it serves,
Or lose our ventures.

William Shakespeare

From STRADIVARIUS

God be praised,
Antonio Stradivari has an eye
That winces at false work and loves the true.
And for my fame—when any master holds
'Twixt chin and hand a violin of mine,
He will be glad that Stradivari lived,
Made violins, and made them of the best . . .

I say not God Himself can make man's best
Without best men to help Him . . .
  'Tis God gives skill,
But not without men's hands: He could not make
Antonio Stradivari's violins
Without Antonio.

George Eliot

From TO A LOUSE

O wad some Power the giftie gie us
To see oursels as ithers see us!
It wad frae monie a blunder free us,
   An' foolish notion.
What airs in dress an' gait wad lea'e us,
An' ev'n devotion!

Robert Burns

WHOSO DRAWS NIGH TO GOD

Whoso draws nigh to God one step
    through doubtings dim,
God will advance a mile
    in blazing light to him.

Author unknown

From "ANDREW RYKMAN'S PRAYER"

If there be some weaker one,
Give me strength to help him on;
If a blinder soul there be,
Let me guide him nearer Thee.
Make my mortal dreams come true
With the work I fain would do;
Clothe with life the weak intent,
Let me be the thing I meant;
Let me find in Thy employ
Peace that dearer is than joy;
Out of self to love be led
And to heaven acclimated,
Until all things sweet and good
Seem my natural habitude.

John Greenleaf Whittier

THE SHEPHERD BOY'S SONG

He that is down needs fear no fall
   He that is low, no pride;
He that is humble ever shall
   Have God to be his guide.

I am content with that I have,
   Little be it or much;
And Lord, contentment still I crave,
   Because Thou savest such.

Fullness to such a burden is
   That go on pilgrimage;
Here little, and hereafter bliss,
   Is best from age to age.

John Bunyan

IF

If I can stop one heart from breaking
   I shall not live in vain;
If I can ease one life the aching
   Or cool one pain,
Or help one fainting robin
   Unto his nest again,
I shall not live in vain.

Emily Dickinson

OVERHEARD IN AN ORCHARD

Said the Robin to the Sparrow;
  "I should really like to know
Why these anxious human beings
  Rush about and worry so."

Said the Sparrow to the Robin:
  "Friend, I think that it must be
That they have no heavenly Father
  Such as cares for you and me."

Elizabeth Cheney

THE LAST DEFILE

"He died climbing"—A Swiss Guide's Epitaph

Make us Thy mountaineers:
We would not linger on the lower slope,
Fill us afresh with hope, O God of Hope,
That undefeated we may climb the hill
As seeing Him who is invisible.

Let us die climbing. When this little while
Lies far behind us, and the last defile
Is all alight, and in that light we see
Our Leader and our Lord, what will it be?

Amy Carmichael

THE WAYS

To every man there openeth
A Way, and Ways, and a Way.
And the High Soul climbs the High Way,
And the Low Soul gropes the Low,
And in between, on the misty flats,
The rest drift to and fro.
But to every man there openeth
A High Way, and a Low.
And every man decideth
The Way his soul shall go.

John Oxenham

From BISHOP BLOUGRAM'S APOLOGY

When the fight begins within himself,
A man's worth something. God stoops o'er his head,
Satan looks up between his feet,—both tug —
He's left, himself, i' the middle: the Soul wakes
And grows. Prolong that battle through his life!
Never leave growing till the life to come!

Robert Browning

FAITH

Nothing before, nothing behind;
    The steps of faith
Fall on the seeming void, and find
    The rock beneath.

John Greenleaf Whittier

DEDICATION

Thou, whose unmeasured temple stands,
    Built over earth and sea,
Accept the walls that human hands
    Have raised, O God, to Thee!

Lord, from Thine inmost glory send,
    Within these courts to bide,
The peace that dwelleth without end
    Serenely by Thy side!

May erring minds that worship here
    Be taught the better way;
And they who mourn, and they who fear,
    Be strengthened as they pray.

May faith grow firm, and love grow warm,
    And pure devotion rise,
While round these hallowed walls the storm
    Of earthborn passion dies.

William Cullen Bryant

ON HIS BLINDNESS

When I consider how my light is spent
Ere half my days in this dark world and wide,
And that one talent which is death to hide
Lodged with me useless, though my soul more bent
To serve therewith my Maker, and present
My true account, lest He returning chide,
"Doth God exact day-labour, light denied?"
I fondly ask. But Patience, to prevent
That murmur, soon replies, "God doth not need
Either man's work or his own gifts. Who best
Bear his mild yoke, they serve Him best. His state
Is kingly: thousands at His bidding speed,
And post o'er land and ocean without rest;
They also serve who only stand and wait."

John Milton

FLOWER IN THE CRANNIED WALL

Flower in the crannied wall,
I pluck you out of the crannies,
I hold you here, root and all, in my hand,
Little flower—but *if* I could understand
What you are, root and all, and all in all,
I should know what God and man is.

Alfred Tennyson

PROPS

Earthly props are useless,
   On Thy grace I fall;
Earthly strength is weakness,
   Father, on Thee I call—
   For comfort, strength, and guidance,
   O, give me all!

John Oxenham

PREVAILING PRAYER

Lord, what a change within us one short hour
Spent in Thy presence will prevail to make!
What heavy burdens from our bosoms take,
What parched grounds revive as with a shower!
We kneel, and all around us seems to lower;
We rise, and all the distant and the near
Stands forth in sunny outline brave and clear;
We kneel, how weak! we rise, how full of power!
Why, therefore, should we do ourselves this wrong,
Or others, that we are not always strong,
That we are ever overborne with care;
That we should ever weak or heartless be,
Anxious or troubled, when with us is prayer,
And joy and strength and courage are with Thee!

Archbishop Trench

PEACE AND JOY

Passionately fierce the voice of God is pleading,
    Pleading with men to arm them for the fight,
See how those hands, majestically bleeding,
    Call us to rout the armies of the night.

Not to the work of sordid selfish saving
    Of our own souls to dwell with Him on high,
But to the soldier's splendid selfless braving,
    Eager to fight for righteousness and die.

Peace does not mean the end of all our striving,
    Joy does not mean the drying of our tears,
Peace is the power that comes to souls arriving
    Up to the light where God Himself appears.

Joy is the wine that God is ever pouring
    Into the hearts of those who strive with Him,
Light'ning their eyes to vision and adoring,
    Strength'ning their arms to warfare glad and grim.

G. A. Studdert-Kennedy

From SIR GALAHAD

    My good blade carves the casques of men,
        My tough lance thrusteth sure,
    My strength is as the strength of ten,
        Because my heart is pure.

Alfred Tennyson

From THE RIME OF THE ANCIENT MARINER

> He prayeth best who loveth best
>   All things both great and small;
> For the dear God who loveth us,
>   He made and loveth all.

Samuel Taylor Coleridge

AN ANGEL UNAWARES

> If after kirk ye bide a wee,
>   There's some would like to speak to ye.
> If after kirk ye rise and flee,
>   We'll all seem cold and stiff to ye.
> That one that's in the seat wi' ye,
>   Is stranger here than you, may be;
> Add you your soul unto our prayers;
>   Be you our angel unawares.

Author unknown

THE WAY

> Who seeks for heaven alone to save his soul
> May keep the path, but will not reach the goal;
> While he who walks in love may wander far,
> Yet God will bring him where the blessed are.

Henry van Dyke

RETRIBUTION

"The mills of the gods grind late, but they grind fine."
Greek poet

Though the mills of God grind slowly,
Yet they grind exceeding small;
Though with patience He stands waiting,
With exactness grinds He all.

Henry Wadsworth Longfellow

THE BOOK OUR MOTHERS READ

We search the world for truth; we cull
The good, the pure, the beautiful,
From graven stone and written scroll,
And all old flower-fields of the soul;
And, weary seekers of the best,
We come back laden from the quest,
To find that all the sages said
Is in the Book our mothers read.

John Greenleaf Whittier

POSSESSION

Heaven above is softer blue
   Earth beneath is sweeter green.
Something lives in every hue,
   Christless eyes have never seen.
Birds with gladder songs o'erflow,
   Flowers with deeper beauty shine
Since I know as now I know
   I am His and He is mine.

Author unknown

BIDE A WEE!

Though the times be dark and dreary,
Though the way be long,
Keep your spirits bright and cheery—
—"Bide a wee, and dinna weary!"
   Is a heartsome song.

John Oxenham

THAT HOLY THING

They all were looking for a king
   To slay their foes and lift them high;
Thou cam'st, a little baby thing
   That made a woman cry.

O son of Man, to right my lot
   Naught but Thy presence can avail;
Yet on the road Thy wheels are not,
   Nor on the sea Thy sail!

My how or when Thou wilt not heed,
   But come down Thine own secret stair,
That Thou mayst answer all my need—
   Yea, every bygone prayer.

George Macdonald

BETRAYAL

   Still as of old
   Men by themselves are priced—
   For thirty pieces Judas sold
   Himself, not Christ.

Hester H. Cholmondeley

INDIFFERENCE

When Jesus came to Golgotha they hanged Him on a tree,
They drave great nails through hands and feet, and made a Calvary;
They crowned Him with a crown of thorns, red were His wounds and deep,
For those were crude and cruel days, and human flesh was cheap.

When Jesus came to Birmingham, they simply passed Him by,
They never hurt a hair of Him, they only let Him die;
For men had grown more tender, and they would not give Him pain,
They only just passed down the street, and left Him in the rain.

Still Jesus cried, "Forgive them, for they know not what they do,"
And still it rained the wintry rain that drenched Him through and through ;
The crowds went home and left the streets without a soul to see,
And Jesus crouched against a wall and cried for Calvary.

G. A. Studdert-Kennedy

FOUR THINGS

Four things a man must learn to do
If he would make his record true:
To think without confusion clearly;
To love his fellow men sincerely;
To act from honest motives purely;
To trust in God and heaven securely.

Henry van Dyke

THE MASTER-PLAYER

An old, worn harp that had been played
Till all its strings were loose and frayed,
Joy, Hate, and Fear, each one essayed,
To play. But each in turn had found
No sweet responsiveness of sound.

Then Love the Master-Player came
With heaving breast and eyes aflame;
The Harp he took all undismayed,
Smote on its strings, still strange to song,
And brought forth music sweet and strong.

Paul Laurence Dunbar

I SAW GOD WASH THE WORLD

I saw God wash the world last night
    With His sweet showers on high,
And then, when morning came, I saw
    Him hang it out to dry.

He washed each tiny blade of grass
    And every trembling tree;
He flung His showers against the hill,
    And swept the billowing sea.

The white rose is a cleaner white,
    The red rose is more red,
Since God washed every fragrant face
    And put them all to bed.

There's not a bird, there's not a bee
    That wings along the way
But is a cleaner bird and bee
    Than it was yesterday.

I saw God wash the world last night.
    Ah, would He had washed me
As clean of all my dust and dirt
    As that old white birch tree.

William L. Stidger

THEY THAT WAIT UPON THE LORD

Hast thou not known?
Hast thou not heard,
   that the everlasting God,
      the Lord,
         the Creator of the ends of the earth,
           fainteth not,
              neither is weary?
   there is no searching of His understanding.

He giveth power to the faint,
   and to them that have no might
      He increaseth strength.

Even the youths shall faint
   and be weary,
      and the young men shall utterly fall.

But they that wait upon the Lord
   shall renew their strength:
      they shall mount up with wings as eagles,
      they shall run and not be weary,
         and they shall walk,
           and not faint.

                              Isaiah 40:28-31

THE DAY'S DEMAND

God give us men! A time like this demands
Strong minds, great hearts, true faith and ready hands;
Men whom the lust of office does not kill;
   Men whom the spoils of office cannot buy:
Men who possess opinions and a will;
   Men who have honor—men who will not lie;
Men who can stand before a demagogue
   And damn his treacherous flatteries without winking,
Tall men, sun-crowned, who live above the fog
   In public duty and in private thinking;
For while the rabble, with their thumb-worn creeds,
Their large professions and their little deeds,
Mingle in selfish strife, lo! Freedom weeps,
Wrong rules the land, and waiting Justice sleeps.

Josiah Gilbert Holland

I AM NOT BOUND TO WIN

I am not bound to win,
But I am bound to be true.
I am not bound to succeed,
But I am bound to live up to what light I have.
I must stand with anybody that stands right;
Stand with him while he is right,
And part with him when he goes wrong.

Abraham Lincoln

RECESSIONAL

God of our fathers, known of old,
   Lord of our far-flung battle line,
Beneath Whose awful hand we hold
   Dominion over palm and pine,
Lord God of Hosts, be with us yet,
Lest we forget—lest we forget!

The tumult and the shouting dies,
   The captains and the kings depart;
Still stands Thine ancient Sacrifice,
   An humble and a contrite heart.
Lord God of Hosts, be with us yet,
Lest we forget—lest we forget!

Far called, our navies melt away,
   On dune and headland sinks the fire;
Lo, all our pomp of yesterday
   Is one with Nineveh and Tyre!
Judge of the Nations, spare us yet,
Lest we forget—lest we forget!

If, drunk with sight of power, we loose
   Wild tongues that have not Thee in awe,
Such boastings as the Gentiles use—
   Or lesser breeds without the law—
Lord God of Hosts, be with us yet,
Lest we forget—lest we forget!

For heathen heart that puts her trust
   In reeking tube and iron shard,
All valiant dust that builds on dust,
   And guarding, calls not Thee to guard,

For frantic boast and foolish word,
Thy mercy on Thy people, Lord!
Amen.

Rudyard Kipling

THE WORLD OVER

In vain we call old notions fudge,
    And bend our conscience to our dealing;
The Ten Commandments will not budge,
    And stealing will continue stealing.

James Russell Lowell

From THE PRESENT CRISIS

Careless seems the great Avenger; history's pages but record
One death-struggle in the darkness 'twixt old systems and the Word;
Truth forever on the scaffold, Wrong forever on the throne,—
Yet that scaffold sways the future, and, behind the dim unknown,
Standeth God within the shadow, keeping watch above His own.

James Russell Lowell

A NATION'S STRENGTH

What makes a nation's pillars high
   And its foundations strong?
What makes it mighty to defy
   The foes that round it throng?

It is not gold. Its kingdoms grand
   Go down in battle shock;
Its shafts are laid on sinking sand,
   Not on abiding rock.

Is it the sword? Ask the red dust
   Of empires passed away;
The blood has turned their stones to rust,
   Their glory to decay.

And is it pride? Ah, that bright crown
   Has seemed to nations sweet;
But God has struck its luster down
   In ashes at His feet.

Not gold but only men can make
   A people great and strong;
Men who for truth and honor's sake
   Stand fast and suffer long.

Brave men who work while others sleep,
   Who dare while others fly—
They build a nation's pillars deep
   And lift them to the sky.

Ralph Waldo Emerson

OUR MASTER

We may not climb the heavenly steeps
   To bring the Lord Christ down;
In vain we search the lowest deeps,
   For Him no depths can drown.

But warm, sweet, tender, even yet
   A present help is He;
And faith has still its Olivet,
   And love its Galilee.

Through Him the first fond prayers are said
   Our lips of childhood frame;
The last low whispers of our dead
   Are burdened with His name.

O Lord and Master of us all,
   Whate'er our name or sign,
We own Thy sway, we hear Thy call,
   We test our lives by Thine!

John Greenleaf Whittier

From ALUMNUS FOOTBALL

For when the One Great Scorer comes
To write against your name,
He writes—not that you won or lost—
But how you played the game.

Grantland Rice

CROSSING THE BAR

Sunset and evening star,
   And one clear call for me!
And may there be no moaning of the bar,
   When I put out to sea,

But such a tide as moving seems asleep,
   Too full for sound and foam,
When that which drew from out the boundless deep
   Turns again home.

Twilight and evening bell,
   And after that the dark!
And may there be no sadness of farewell,
   When I embark;

For tho' from out our bourne of Time and Place
   The flood may bear me far,
I hope to see my Pilot face to face
   When I have crost the bar.

Alfred Tennyson

WINGS

Let us be like a bird for a moment perched
   On a frail branch while he sings;
Though he feels it bend, yet he sings his song,
   Knowing that he has wings.

Victor Hugo

VANISHED

She died—this is the way she died;
   And when her breath was done,
Took up her simple wardrobe
   And started for the sun.

Her little figure at the gate
   The angels must have spied,
Since I could never find her
   Upon the mortal side.

Emily Dickinson

From THE ETERNAL GOODNESS

I know not what the future hath
   Of marvel or surprise,
Assured alone that life and death,
   His mercy underlies:

And so beside the Silent Sea
   I wait the muffled oar;
No harm from Him can come to me
   On ocean or on shore.

I know not where His islands lift
   Their fronded palms in air;
I only know I cannot drift
   Beyond His love and care.

John Greenleaf Whittier

From THE CHAMBERED NAUTILUS

Build thee more stately mansions, O my soul,
   As the swift seasons roll!
   Leave thy low-vaulted past!
Let each new temple, nobler than the last,
Shut thee from heaven with a dome more vast,
   Till thou at length art free,
Leaving thine outgrown shell by life's unresting sea!

Oliver Wendell Holmes

From RABBI BEN EZRA

Grow old along with me!
The best is yet to be,
The last of life, for which the first was made:
Our times are in His hand
Who saith "A whole I planned,
Youth shows but half; trust God: see all, nor be afraid!"

Robert Browning

ON HIS SEVENTY-FIFTH BIRTHDAY

I strove with none; for none was worth my strife,
    Nature I loved, and next to Nature, Art;
I warmed both hands before the fire of life,
    It sinks, and I am ready to depart.

Walter Savage Landor

SIR WALTER RALEIGH'S VERSES, FOUND IN HIS BIBLE IN THE GATEHOUSE AT WESTMINSTER

Even such is time, that takes in trust
Our youth, our joys, our all we have,
And pays us but with age and dust;
Who in the dark and silent grave,
When we have wandered all our ways,
Shuts up the story of our days.
But from this earth, this grave, this dust,
My God shall raise me up, I trust!

Walter Raleigh

DEATH

Death, be not proud, though some have called thee
Mighty and dreadful, for thou art not so:
For those whom thou think'st thou dost overthrow
Die not, poor Death; nor yet canst thou kill me.

From rest and sleep, which but thy picture be,
Much pleasure; then from thee much more must flow;
And soonest our best men with thee do go—
Rest of their bones and souls' delivery!
Thou'rt slave to fate, chance, kings, and desperate men,
And dost with poison, war, and sickness dwell;
And poppy or charms can make us sleep as well
And better than thy stroke. Why swell'st thou then?
   One short sleep past, we wake eternally,
   And Death shall be no more: Death, thou shalt die!

John Donne

From ULYSSES

I am a part of all that I have met;
Yet all experience is an arch wherethro'
Gleams that untravell'd world whose margin fades
For ever and for ever when I move.
How dull it is to pause, to make an end,
To rust unburnish'd, not to shine in use!
As tho' to breathe were life! Life piled on life
Were all too little, and of one to me
Little remains; but every hour is saved
From that eternal silence, something more,
A bringer of new things; and vile it were
For some three suns to store and hoard myself,
And this gray spirit yearning in desire
To follow knowledge like a sinking star,
Beyond the utmost bound of human thought.

Alfred Tennyson

From THE OLD ASTRONOMER

Though my soul may set in darkness, it will rise in perfect light,
I have loved the stars too fondly to be fearful of the night.

Sarah Williams

EPITAPH PLACED ON HIS DAUGHTER'S TOMB BY MARK TWAIN

Warm summer sun,
Shine kindly here.
Warm southern wind,
Blow softly here.

Green sod above,
Lie light, lie light.
Good night, dear heart,
Good night, good night.

*Adapted from
Robert Richardson*

REQUIEM

Under the wide and starry sky
    Dig the grave and let me die:
Glad did I live and gladly die,
    And I laid me down with a will.

This be the verse you grave for me:
Here he lies where he longed to be:
Home is the sailor, home from sea,
And the hunter home from the hill.

                  Robert Louis Stevenson

MUSIC, WHEN SOFT VOICES DIE

Music, when soft voices die,
Vibrates in the memory —
Odours, when sweet violets sicken,
Live within the sense they quicken.

Rose leaves, when the rose is dead,
Are heap'd for the beloved's bed;
And so thy thoughts, when thou art gone,
Love itself shall slumber on.

                  Percy Bysshe Shelley